An Educational Activity/Coloring Book

BIRD MAZES

Created by
Peter M. Spizzirri

This Is An Educational/Activity Coloring Book of BIRD MAZES • Published by SPIZZIRRI PUBLISHING, INC., P.O. BOX 9397, RAPID CITY, SOUTH DAKOTA 57709. No part of this publication may be reproduced, stored in a retrievable system, or transmitted in any form without the express written consent of the publisher. All national and international rights reserved on the entire contents of this publication.
Printed in U.S.A.

The Birds In This Book Are Different Sizes

Bird Name	Length	Bird Name	Length
Barn Swallow	5 to 7 inches	Red-Headed Woodpecker	7 1/2 inches
Black Crowned Night Heron	23 to 26 inches	Rose-Breasted Grosbeak	7 inches
Cedar Waxwing	5 to 7 inches	Screech Owl	7 to 10 inches
Cooper's Hawk	15 1/2 inches	Song Sparrow	7 to 8 inches
Crow	16 to 20 inches	Sparrow Hawk	8 1/2 inches
Curve-Billed Thrasher	10 inches	Spotted Sandpiper	7 to 8 inches
Emperor Penguin	4 feet	Steller's Jay	11 to 13 inches
Great Blue Heron	30 to 40 inches	Winter Wren	3 to 4 inches
Mallard Duck	16 to 24 inches	Wood Duck	18 to 21 inches
Painted Bunting	5 to 51/2 inchess	Woodcock	10 to 12 inches
		Yellow Billed Magpie	16 inches

Painted Bunting

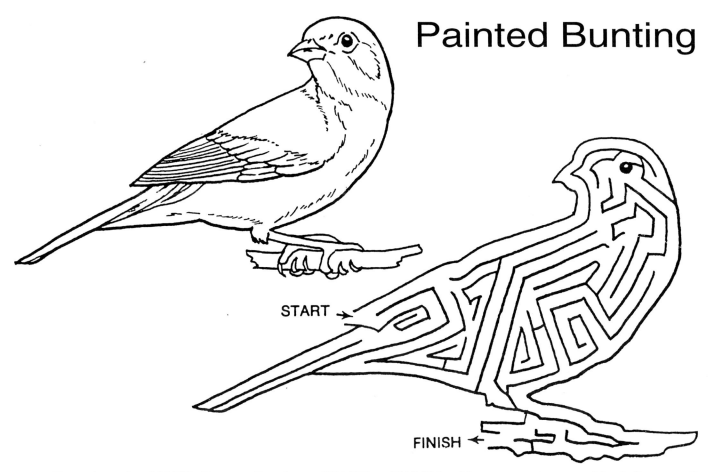

START →

FINISH ←

Complete the MAZE. Draw a line from START to FINISH, without crossing any black lines. **3**

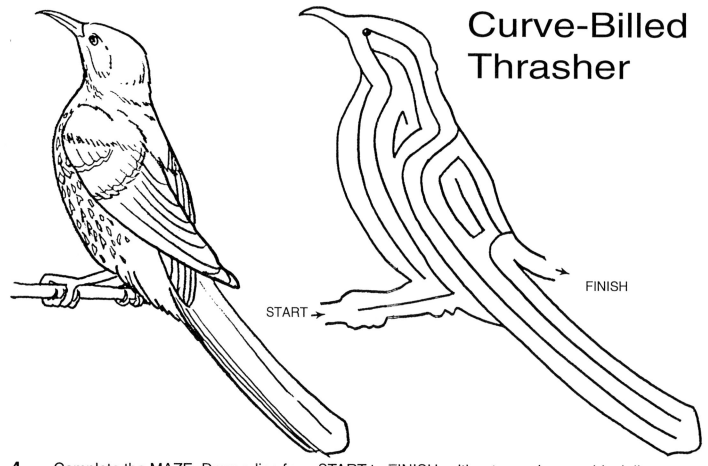

Curve-Billed Thrasher

START →

FINISH

4   Complete the MAZE. Draw a line from START to FINISH, without crossing any black lines.

Barn Swallow

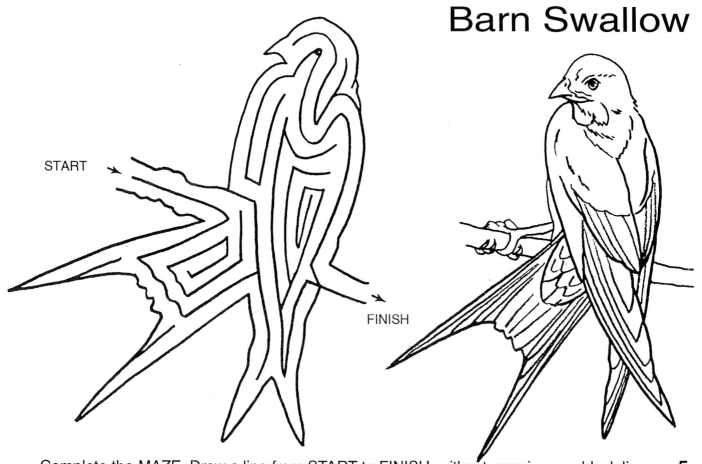

START

FINISH

Complete the MAZE. Draw a line from START to FINISH, without crossing any black lines. **5**

Red-Headed Woodpecker

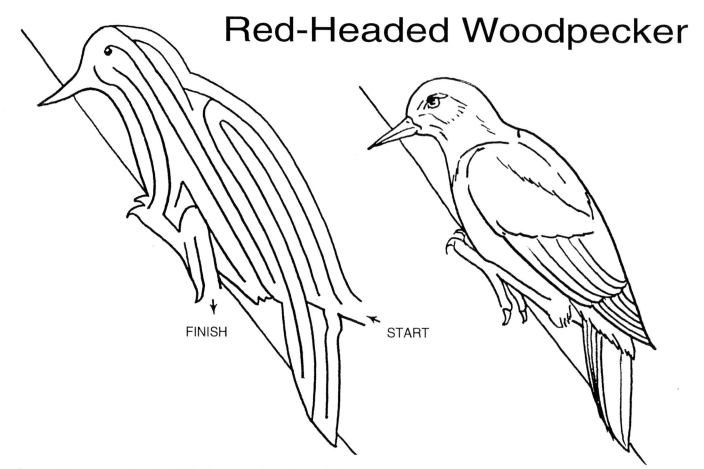

FINISH

START

6   Complete the MAZE. Draw a line from START to FINISH, without crossing any black lines.

Rose-Breasted Grosbeak

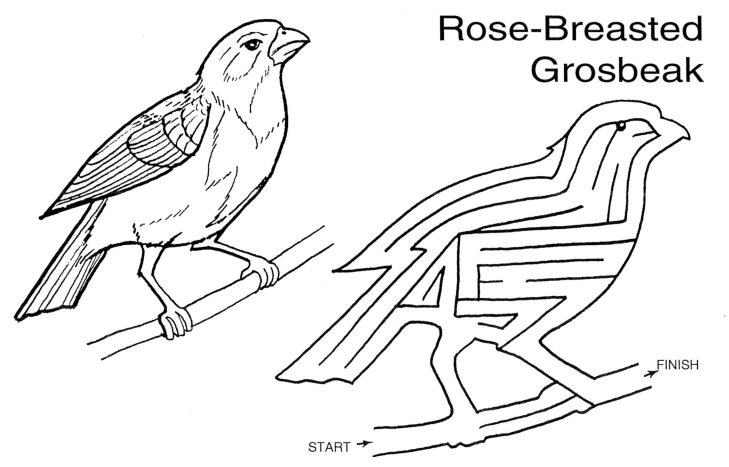

FINISH

START

Complete the MAZE. Draw a line from START to FINISH, without crossing any black lines. **7**

Crow

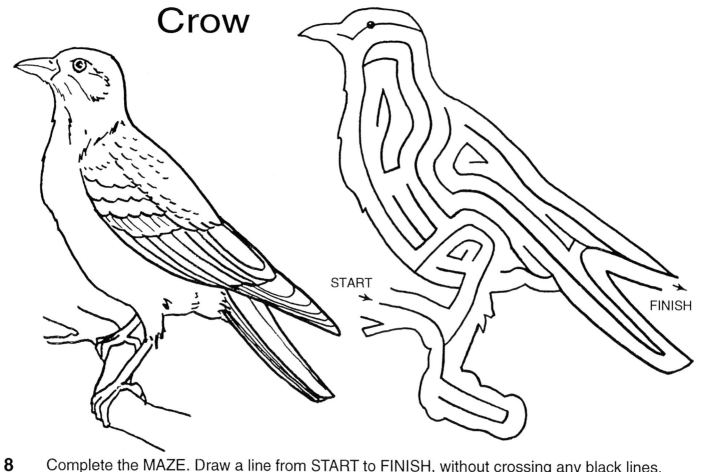

START

FINISH

8   Complete the MAZE. Draw a line from START to FINISH, without crossing any black lines.

Yellow Billed Magpie

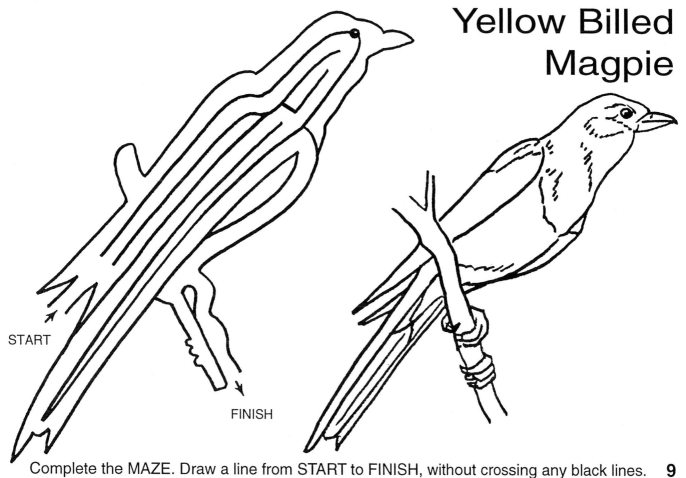

START

FINISH

Complete the MAZE. Draw a line from START to FINISH, without crossing any black lines. **9**

Great Blue Heron

START

FINISH ←

10 Complete the MAZE. Draw a line from START to FINISH, without crossing any black lines.

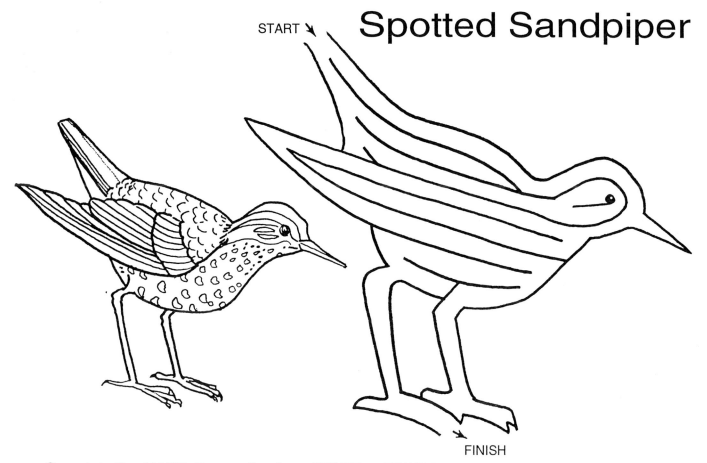

START

Spotted Sandpiper

FINISH

Complete the MAZE. Draw a line from START to FINISH, without crossing any black lines. **11**

Wood Duck

START

FINISH

12 Complete the MAZE. Draw a line from START to FINISH, without crossing any black lines.

Steller's Jay

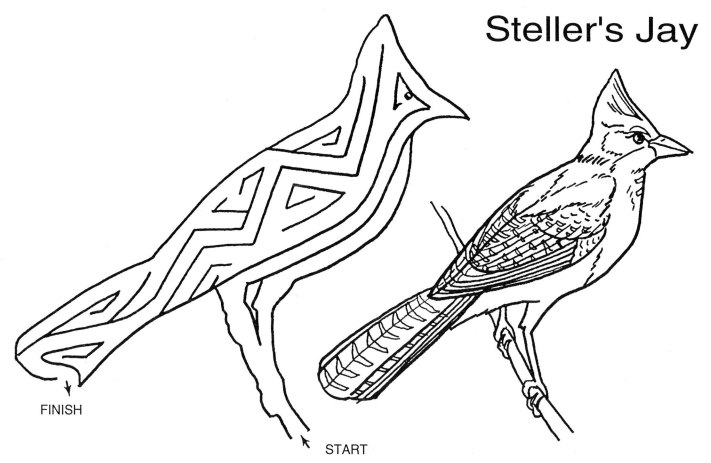

FINISH

START

Complete the MAZE. Draw a line from START to FINISH, without crossing any black lines. **13**

Black-Crowned Night Heron

FINISH

START

14 Complete the MAZE. Draw a line from START to FINISH, without crossing any black lines.

START

Screech Owl

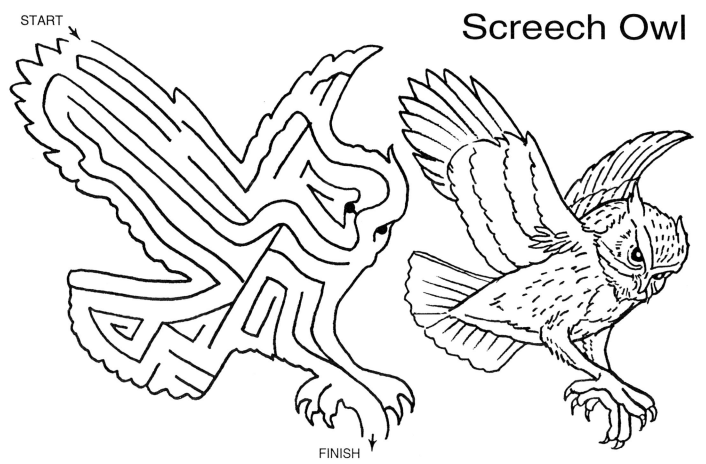

FINISH

Complete the MAZE. Draw a line from START to FINISH, without crossing any black lines. **15**

Song Sparrow

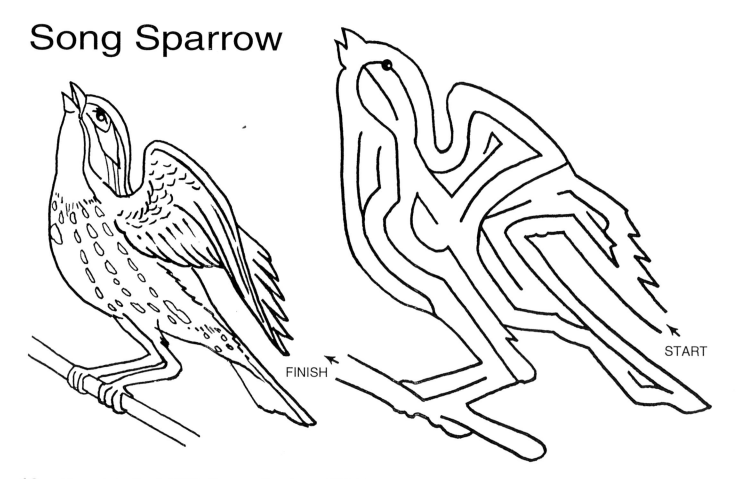

FINISH

START

16 Complete the MAZE. Draw a line from START to FINISH, without crossing any black lines.

Mallard Duck

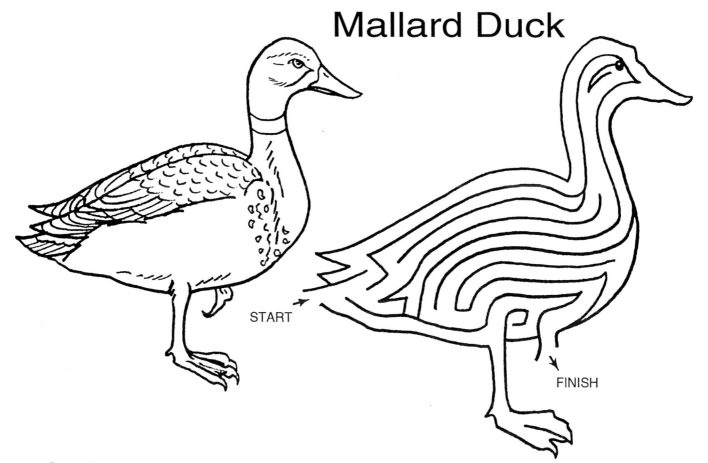

START

FINISH

Complete the MAZE. Draw a line from START to FINISH, without crossing any black lines. **17**

Woodcock

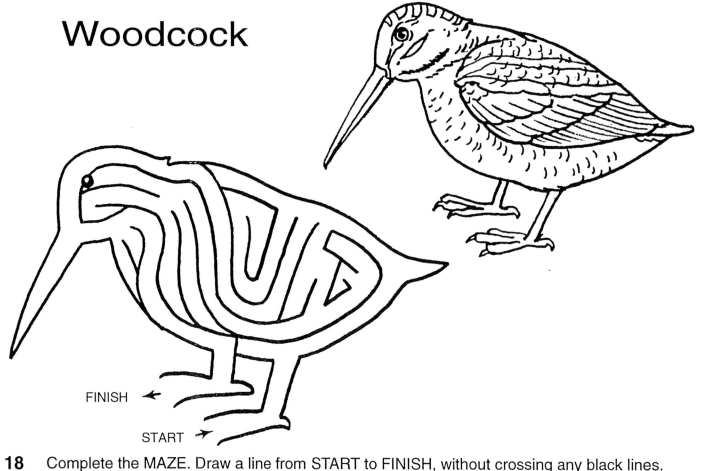

FINISH ←

START →

18   Complete the MAZE. Draw a line from START to FINISH, without crossing any black lines.

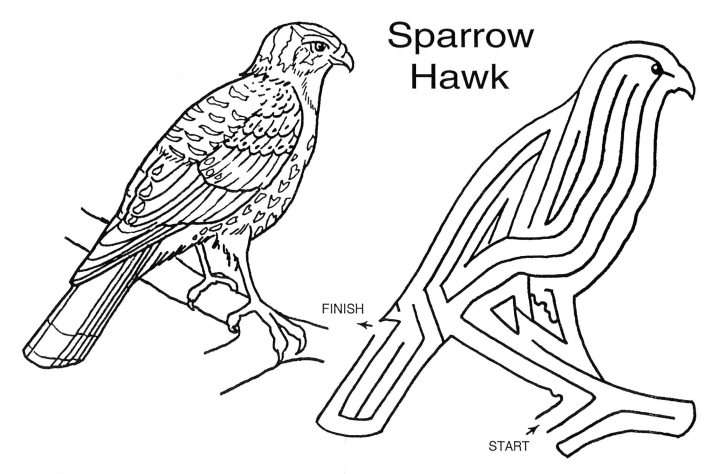

Sparrow Hawk

FINISH

START

Complete the MAZE. Draw a line from START to FINISH, without crossing any black lines.   **19**

Emperor Penguin

START

FINISH ←

20   Complete the MAZE. Draw a line from START to FINISH, without crossing any black lines.

FINISH ↑

Winter Wren

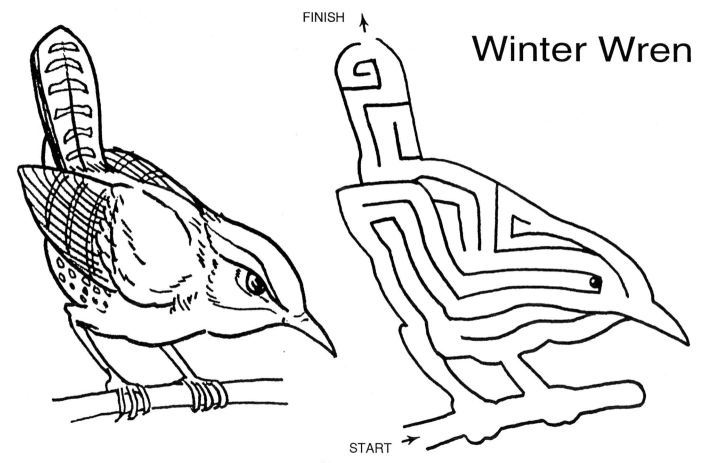

START →

Complete the MAZE. Draw a line from START to FINISH, without crossing any black lines. **21**

Cedar Waxwing

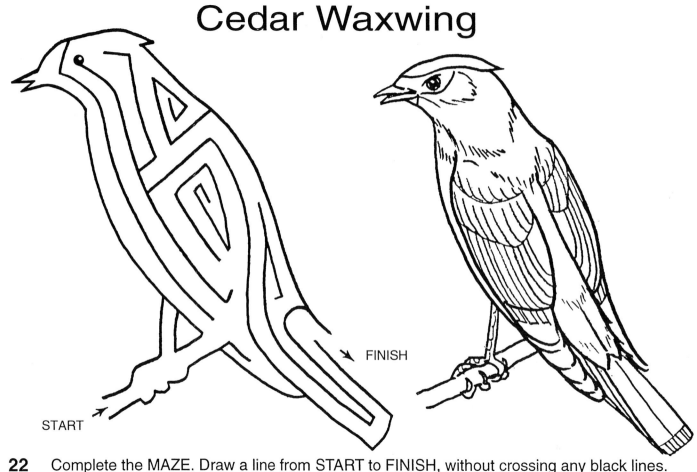

START

FINISH

22 Complete the MAZE. Draw a line from START to FINISH, without crossing any black lines.

Cooper's Hawk

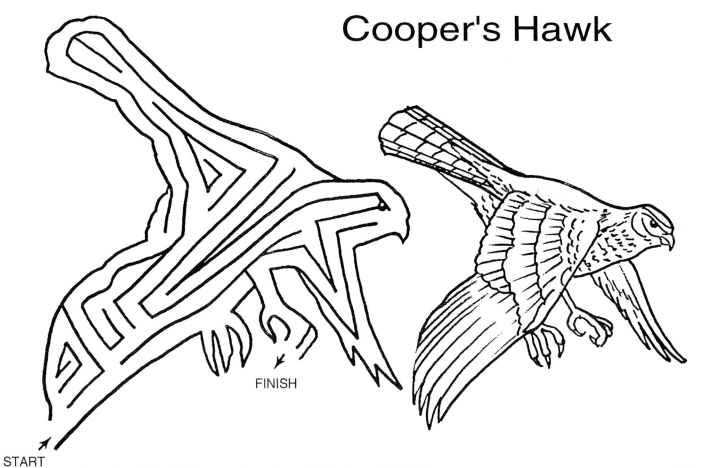

START

FINISH

Complete the MAZE. Draw a line from START to FINISH, without crossing any black lines.   23

OTHER CHILDREN'S BOOKS CREATED BY SPIZZIRRI PUBLISHING

ISBN (INTERNATIONAL STANDARD BOOK NUMBER) PREFIX ON ALL SPIZZIRRI BOOKS IS: 0-86545-

EDUCATIONAL READ AND COLOR BOOKS

ILLUSTRATIONS AND TEXT
SIZE: 8 1/2" X 11"

AIRCRAFT
ANIMAL ALPHABET
ANIMAL F. CALENDAR
ANIMAL GIANTS
ATLANTIC FISH
AUTOMOBILES
BIRDS
CALIFORNIA INDIANS
CALIFORNIA MISSIONS
CATS
CATS OF THE WILD
CAVE MAN
COLONIES
COMETS
Count/Color DINOSAURS
COWBOYS
DEEP-SEA FISH
DINOSAURS
DINOSAURS OF PREY
DOGS
DOGS OF THE WILD
DOLLS
DOLPHINS
EAGLES
ENDANGERED BIRDS
Endang'd Mam'ls-AFRICA

Endang'd Mam'ls- ASIA & CHINA
Endang'd Mam'ls-SO. AMERICA
ENDANGERED SPECIES
ESKIMOS
FARM ANIMALS
FISH
HORSES
KACHINA DOLLS
LAUTREC POSTERS
MAMMALS
MARINE MAMMALS
MARSUPIALS
NORTHEAST INDIANS
NORTHWEST INDIANS
PACIFIC FISH
PALEOZOIC LIFE
PENGUINS
PICTURE CROSSWORDS
PICTURE DICTIONARY
PIONEERS
PLAINS INDIANS
PLANETS
POISONOUS SNAKES
Prehist. BIRDS
Prehist. FISH
Prehist. MAMMALS
Prehist. SEA LIFE
PRIMATES

RAIN FOREST BIRDS
RAIN FOREST RIVER LIFE
RAIN FOREST TREE LIFE
REPTILES
ROCKETS
SATELLITES
SHARKS
SHIPS
SHUTTLE CRAFT
SOUTHEAST INDIANS
SOUTHWEST INDIANS
SPACE CRAFT
SPACE EXPLORERS
STATE BIRDS
STATE FLOWERS
TEXAS
TRANSPORTATION
TRUCKS
WHALES

SILHOUETTE ART BOOKS
8 1/2 x 11" Reproducible

CHRISTMAS
CIRCUS
DINOSAURS
FARM ANIMALS
OCEAN LIFE
ZOO ANIMALS

EDUCATIONAL ACTIVITY BOOKS
SIZE: 5 1/2 x 8 1/2"

Alphabet Dot-to-dot PETS
Alphabet Dot-to-dot ZOO ANIMALS
BIRD MAZES
BUTTERFLY MAZES
DINOSAUR MAZES
Dot-to-dot DINOSAURS
Dot-to-dot FISH
Dot-to-dot REPTILES
Dot-to-dot WHALES
FARM MAZES
FISH MAZES
FLOWER MAZES
MAMMAL MAZES
SHARK MAZES
SHELL MAZES
TREE MAZES
TURTLE MAZES
ZOO MAZES

Educational FACTS and FUN Books
SIZE: 5 1/2 X 8 1/2"

ANIMAL LEAPS
ANIMAL SPEEDS
ANIMALS THAT LAY EGGS
ANIMALS WITH LONG NECKS
ANIMALS WITH LONG TAILS
BIRD SPEEDS

FOOTPRINTS OF BIRDS
INSECT HUNTERS
MAMMAL FOOTPRINTS
POISONOUS ANIMALS
SKATES AND RAYS
SMALL MAMMALS

EARLY LEARNING WORKBOOKS
SIZE: 8 1/2 x 11"

ALPHABET PICTURES
COMPLETE THE WORDS
COUNTING DINOSAURS
Dot to dot ALPHABET
Dot to dot NUMBERS
FIRST ADDITION
FIRST ALPHABET
FIRST NUMBERS
FIRST SUBTRACTION
MAKE A CALENDAR
MAKING WORDS
MAZE PUZZLES
NUMBERS and COLORS
PICTURE CROSSWORDS
PICTURE DICTIONARY
SHAPES, ART & COLORS
THEY GO TOGETHER
TRIANGLE PICTURES
WORD HUNT PUZZLES
WORDS IN WORDS